# Chatur Demystifies Banking

I0393565

Vikram Viswanathan

INDIA · SINGAPORE · MALAYSIA

## Notion Press

No.8, 3rd Cross Street,
CIT Colony, Mylapore,
Chennai, Tamil Nadu – 600004

First Published by Notion Press 2020
Copyright © Vikram Viswanathan 2020
All Rights Reserved.

ISBN 978-1-63669-711-6

# Dedication

This book is dedicated to Manjula
Viswanathan, K. Viswanathan and V. Vidya

# Contents

# Foreword

The objective of writing this book is to demystify and simplify a few core concepts in the world of banking. The type of banking-related terminology and jargon that we encounter frequently in newspapers and other sources is simply mindboggling. Many of us are not only dazed and confused by such complex jargon but also start assuming, perhaps wrongly, that this subject is not for lesser mortals.

In reality, most topics become easy to understand, once we explain using very simple examples. This is what this book aims and hopes to achieve when it comes to the fundamentals of banking. In fact, you can argue that if one cannot explain something, which everyone can easily understand, then that person perhaps does not understand that subject that well.

In this book, we will try to answer the following basic questions in simple and easily understandable terms.

- What is the meaning of intermediation?

- Why do banks pay interest income to depositors?

- What is the meaning of capital adequacy, NPAs and net interest margins?

- Why do banks need branches when virtually everything can be done online?

- How do banks make money from credit cards?

We will follow our hero "Chatur," who comes into the banking world with absolutely no background. However, he works hard, is innovative and is constantly trying to learn and improve. A series of conversations about different aspects of banking forms the backbone of this book.

# Acknowledgements

Lakshmi Sangam

Arya Vikram

# Chatur and Bachat Bank

Chatur hails from a typical low-income family and is born and brought up in a small village. His parents are farmers and his family consists of six members, including three of his siblings. As far as his schooling was concerned, Chatur stopped at pre-university level because he had no conviction whatsoever in classroom learning.

He believed he could learn a lot more from observation, exploration and experience rather than from pure bookish knowledge. It was entirely due to his parents' insistence that he even managed to complete pre-university education.

But make no mistake; Chatur is a street-smart, shrewd and very practical individual. By nature, he is curious, inquisitive, and always absorbing new things like a fresh sponge. These attributes help him to quickly learn, grasp and understand new concepts. He always dreams of living life king-size, is extremely ambitious and more importantly, has a big heart to chase down those dreams.

However, Chatur's dad is the exact opposite of him – he is very conservative, content and safe in his own comfort zone. Chatur had seen his father forgo many opportunities, which went literally begging. There was this one instance, which he never forgot even until today. The local bank was ready to finance new farm equipment at subsidized interest rates. The bankers had even come to Chatur's home to disburse the loan. They knew that his family owned farm land and this equipment had the ability to increase productivity and improve farm yields multifold. However, Chatur's father chose to look at the risks and travails of borrowing completely overlooking its benefits.

The bankers had explained that they had to maintain a certain portion of loan book in priority sector lending according to banking rules and regulations. Therefore, this loan could help them meet that criteria and would be a win-win situation for both the lender and the borrower. The Government considers farm loans as priority sector loans.

Chatur knew that the bankers has been right about this and that it had the potential to take their family to a different plateau. Moreover, the dynamics of a farm loan did not escape his attention. He guessed correctly that since this was a farm loan, if something went wrong there was a good chance of a bailout. Political parties running for elections often use bailouts as a populist measure. What better populist measure than waiving farm loans? However, try as he might, he could not convince his father on this.

Chatur was aware that perception about risk varied amongst people and was shaped by upbringing, experiences and knowledge, amongst other things.

Anyway, after finishing his pre-university education, he works for a few months as an accountant to earn some extra income, but his heart is not there. Chatur concludes that he would have to move on from his village if he has to accomplish anything note-worthy. After much resistance from his family and after a long debate with his father, he finally leaves for the city.

Once he reaches the city, he obtains the job of a cashier with a well-known bank called "Bachat Bank." His friend, Kuber, who comes from the same village, is the branch manager, which makes things a lot easier for Chatur. Kuber is a taskmaster and a no-nonsense person but Chatur really enjoys working with him. Chatur's first job is to collect money from depositing customers and pay money to withdrawing customers – the job of a cashier.

Kuber is quite impressed with Chatur's efforts. There is not a single error in cash balances in the first six months after Chatur takes over – a marked improvement from the performance of the earlier cashier. Customers are also happy with the speed and quality of service provided by Chatur.

Chatur's ace was that he would always challenge the status quo and bring about changes, which could improve quality and productivity. For example, when he became cashier, he noticed that one-third of the customers who would come to his desk were non-cash customers. Once they reached his desk, they would waste his time in asking a hundred different questions, which he had no time to answer. Their service requirement was entirely different and they were wasting both his and their time. Therefore, he decided to draw and hang up a large placard, which announced that his desk was "Cash only." The placard also displayed coins and notes, which conveyed the message loud and clear. This instantly reduced the number of non-cash customers, thereby increasing his productivity. This measure was so popular that other desks started to copy and implement the same.

Another example was the cash-counting machine, which is the most important machine on a cashier's desk. Chatur noticed that this machine would often break down, creating confusion and lengthening the customer waiting line at his desk. So one day, he sat down with the IT person after office hours to figure out how this situation can be corrected. The IT person opened the cash machine and examined each part, which took nearly two hours, and then explained to Chatur that a couple of missing pins was the root cause of the nagging issue. Chatur brought with him those pins the next day by paying from his own pocket and the machine never troubled him again. He knew getting these things through official channels was time consuming and not very efficient. Such proactive initiatives improved service quality manifold.

What also impresses Kuber is that Chatur was willing to work hard, think smart and keep learning. It was becoming clear to Kuber that Chatur would go a long way within the bank. After office hours, Chatur would spend a lot of time with Kuber and other colleagues to understand about other departments in the bank. He had the rare ability of looking at the big picture as well as focusing on attention to detail.

# The Tales of Badaa and Chotu Shankar

One day Chatur asks Kuber an interesting question. He asks him what happens to all the money that customers deposit with them. Kuber replies saying that the bank lends this money out to borrowers. Chatur then wonders why these depositors cannot directly lend to those borrowers. Why does the bank have to act as an intermediary?

Kuber explains, "You are as naïve as I was a few years back. Nevertheless, it is a very good question. I can tell you that banks perform an important function called "intermediation." They intermediate between savers and borrowers. However, this would be an answer straight from the textbook and too simplistic. Therefore, let me try to explain the concept through some examples. Let me tell you my own experience in lending money to people."

Kuber was an extrovert, outgoing and a socially active person. When he had come to the city, he had quickly developed a strong network of friends and acquaintances with whom he had actively been in touch. One day, one of his friends had casually mentioned to him that a person named Badaa Shankar was desperately looking to borrow money. This aroused Kuber's interest, given that he had been looking to deploy the money that he had saved. His friend had introduced him to Badaa and they had agreed to meet up.

Kuber starts explaining to Chatur the story about Badaa.

Badaa was a round, fat bloke who lived in a good neighborhood and seemed to enjoy a grand life style. He was a person who loved to move on with time and ensured he had all the latest mobile phones, gadgets and what not. Badaa ran a company called Big Impex Private Limited, which traded in different kinds of goods and services, importing and exporting to multiple countries. However, the business was volatile and many a time Badaa faced cash flow-related issues. In fact, he was in one of those dire situations then.

Badaa explained to Kuber about his family, his company and his business operations. He had taken over the business from his dad and expanded it quite a bit. He knew a lot about the trading business, which Kuber was fascinated to listen to and understand. After a long conversation and after many cups of tea, Badaa had finally come to the point.

Badaa "My company recently delivered a large shipment to a client in Africa. This client has deep pockets, has many diversified businesses, and carries a great family name and reputation. We have done business with them over the last ten years and always received payments on time and faced no issues whatsoever.

However, this time there is an unexpected civil war in that African country due to which our shipment is stuck at the port. Therefore, the client is unable to take delivery and with this, a significant amount of our money is locked up, as this was an unusually large shipment.

In the meanwhile, we cannot stop making payments to our own vendors. We approached our bank to let us borrow money to help us come out of this crisis. However, they informed us that we are above the borrowing limit and that they cannot lend us any further money, except if we could put in more collateral."

Kuber "I am so sorry about your shipment. But what is a borrowing limit and what is collateral?"

Badaa "A borrowing limit is the maximum amount of money a bank will lend to a company or an individual. For example, they may set an individual's borrowing limit at six times his monthly salary. To illustrate, if a person's salary is 20,000 rupees a month, he cannot borrow more than 120,000 rupees. He can only increase the borrowing limit if his salary were to increase. If in the following year his salary increases to 25,000 rupees, he can borrow up to 150,000 rupees – an additional 30,000 rupees.

For corporate borrowers, banks will set the borrowing limit after going through the company's financial statements, company's position in the industry, competition levels, its credit history and many other factors.

A collateral is a form of security provided by the borrower to the bank. A simple example is that of a pawnbroker who will not lend you money unless you pledge your gold chain with him. The collateral accepted by the bank includes real estate, stocks and shares, bank deposits and even gold. If the borrower is not able to repay the loan, the bank will seize the collateral, sell it and recover its money.

Banks will maintain a margin of safety when they collateralize a loan. If the loan amount is 100 rupees, they may collect collateral worth 120 rupees or even 150 rupees in some cases. This will protect the bank if there is a decline in the value of that collateral. The loan amount divided by the value of the collateral is equal to the loan-value ratio. The lower the loan to value ratio, the better it is for the banks."

Kuber "Thank you so much for explaining these terms."

Badaa "No problem, my pleasure. I have already pledged my house to the bank and I have no further collateral to provide. In the meanwhile, I have to settle payments to our vendors from whom I have to procure things in order meet a delivery in Singapore. This is the reason I require the money and I am willing to pay an interest rate higher than bank deposit rate."

Kuber "I am more than happy to help. What kind of money are you expecting?"

Badaa "We would need at least 1 crore rupees to make those payments."

Kuber "Badaa sir, I don't have so much money. But I can lend you about 20% of that amount."

Badaa "Kuber, I appreciate your help here. However, that is not good enough and I do not want to deal with multiple small lenders because it is a hassle to cope with so much documentation and multiple contracts. Besides, if I am not able to garner the remaining amount, most likely I may not be able to service the contract. I, then, will not be able to pay interest on your loan as well."

Kuber "Sir, I understand. I hope you are able to get your money soon. I will take your leave then."

Kuber explains to Chatur that eventually Badaa had managed to provide his in-laws' house as collateral and had managed to secure a bank loan against it. On top of this, he also had to pledge some of his family jewelry.

As far as Kuber was concerned, his next target had been Chotu Shankar, one of his acquaintances who was badly in need of money. Chotu was a short thin man who lived in a neighborhood, which did not seem affluent. The day that Kuber had decided to meet him, it was raining cats and dogs.

It was the peak of the monsoon season, and it gave Chotu the perfect opportunity to complain and grumble about the rain. Kuber found it surprising that this man was complaining so much about rain when everyone else was worried about the lack of it and rejoiced at the sight of it.

Anyway, he soon found the real reason behind such anguish. Chotu's concrete roof had been eroded by the constant pounding of the rain and required some serious repair work. However, Chotu did not have the resources to get the work done. In fact, this is the reason he had wanted to borrow some money. He explained to Kuber that he required about 10% of the money that Kuber had saved.

This time around, Kuber faced the opposite issue. The amount of money Chotu wanted to borrow was much smaller compared to Kuber's savings and Kuber was not willing to deal with multiple borrowers. Kuber apologized to Chotu for not being able to give him the money. He, however, advised Chotu to seek a bank loan.

Chotu was aware of bank lending but was apprehensive of the paperwork and time taken to process the loan. However, with help from Kuber – who had just started working for Bachat Bank – he was able to get hold of a loan and managed to plug those horrendous holes in the roof.

Kuber "Chatur, do you see the main issue here? The money that I was willing to lend did not match the money that Badaa and Chotu expected to borrow?"

Chatur "I see that."

Kuber "However, this is not an issue that a bank is going to face, This is because a bank can lend to large as well as small borrowers as it is able to accumulate money from various sources.

Imagine thousands of small streams merging into a big river like Ganga. A bank is exactly similar to this. Except that small savings replace water streams, and form into a massive reservoir made of millions of deposit accounts. This kind of money aggregation enables banks to borrow small and large deposits and also lend to small and large borrowers."

Chatur "That is clear. Thank you."

Kuber "Wait, we are not finished yet on intermediation. Let us continue tomorrow if you don't mind."

Chatur "Sure."

# Kuber's Misery Continues with Udao, Diwaaliya and Dheri

The next day Kuber and Chatur again convene in the evening after office hours.

Kuber continues, "So, by now you know that I could not lend money to either Badaa nor Chotu Shankar. Therefore, I started scouting for other targets. A few days later, one of my friends introduced me to Udao Kumar. Udao was a fashionable young man, looked suave and modern. He was always sporting expensive Gucci T shirts, ultra-modern shades and high-quality sneakers."

During a casual conversation with Kuber, Udao started chatting about the latest imported car in town and how dearly he wanted to buy it. He spent nearly half an hour raving about this car and all the attractions that it offered. However, Udao seemed to be short of cash and the cost of the car happened to match Kuber's savings.

Kuber "Chatur, I sensed an opportunity here and felt excited about finally having met a person who wanted to borrow the exact amount of money that I had saved. However, after my initial excitement wore down, I started to re-think about Udao. He seemed like a spendthrift and careless about spending money, and I began to wonder if this guy would ever repay my money.

I started to make some enquiries and learnt that Udao changed cars and bikes more frequently than his clothes! He had a tendency to borrow money from several people; however, his credit history was extremely poor. He rarely repaid money in time and several times did not repay at all. I, then, began to worry about return of my investment rather than return on my investment. After much deliberation, I decided to pass the opportunity.

Udao failed to get a loan from any of his friends and finally approached a bank asking for an auto loan. The bank asked him to put down 30% of the car value as down payment and agreed to finance the loan, provided he hypothecated the car to the bank."

Chatur "Please can you explain hypothecation?"

Kuber "Hypothecation is a mechanism where banks lend money on the back of owning an asset – in this case, the car. The ownership of the car will remain with the bank until Udao fully repays the bank. If the loan is not repaid in full, the bank will seize the car and then sell it. They will retain whatever is due to them and pay the remaining amount to Udao."

Chatur "But why should they pay anything at all to Udao?"

Kuber "Good question. Let us assume Udao defaults three years after taking the loan. In such a case, he would already have repaid a part of the loan amount. I mean during the three years he would have paid the bank in monthly instalments, which needs to be taken into account.

Let us take an example, which will make it clearer. Let us assume that the loan amount is 100 rupees and also assume that Udao has already repaid 50 rupees. This means only the remaining 50 rupees is due from him. If the bank is able to sell the car for 70 rupees, they will settle the 50 rupees that Udao owes them and then pay the remaining 20 rupees to Udao.

Now let us try to understand how banks solve the issues that I encountered with Udao. The type of functions that banks perform to solve the issue, which I encountered with Udao, is known as 'credit appraisal or underwriting.'

Remember how I found about Udao's credit history through my friends network by sheer luck. Banks do their fact finding in a more much systematic manner. They will employ a team who will do complete due diligence on every potential borrower before they lend him money.

They will go through the bank statements and demand a salary certificate. In addition, they will also check if the company where the person is employed is under the approved list of companies. This is because if the company itself were to get into distress, employees may lose their jobs and then default on their respective loans. The process through which banks decide whether to approve or reject a loan application is also known as underwriting. Sounds like a complex word but very simple, as we just understood.

Banks will also lend money to companies for various business-related activities using the deposits that they receive. This is not easy to achieve for small savers. They will have to understand each and every company's business activities and its future prospects before they lend, which will consume a lot time and resources. It is easier for banks to do this as they have the required resources and systems to do a complete due diligence on a wide variety of companies."

Kuber continues, "Despite all the checks and balances, will all borrowers repay money? Of course, not – some will default. Will banks chase all defaulting borrowers? Of course, yes. They have a team that is dedicated to money collection and recoveries. This team will go after every borrower who did not repay bank money.

However, if the recoveries team is not successful in getting the money back, the legal team will take over and start court proceedings. As you can see, bank has the organizational set-up, the processes and resources to chase and recover money. We cannot expect small savers to have similar systems.

Anyway, my quest to find the right borrower continued. After a few days, I managed to find Dheri Khan, whose requirement seemed to match my savings.

This time I had double-checked and Dheri Khan ticked all the boxes – he was a god-fearing and an honest man and hardly spent money on unnecessary things. Even at the time, he was borrowing money to meet certain emergency medical expenses for his family.

However, to my dismay, Dheri told me that he would require at least five years to repay my money, given his income levels. But I wanted to get my money back with interest in the next 24 months and, therefore, the loan duration that Dheri wanted did not match my expectation."

Chatur "OK, so here we have a mismatch in the loan duration expected between the lender and the borrower."

Kuber "That is correct. Let me explain how banks solve this problem. They collect money over multiple duration from multiple depositors. You may keep your money in a two-year fixed deposit while another person may keep his money over a ten-year fixed deposit. Banks will also lend to multiple borrowers over multiple duration. This sort of mixture will enable banks to match the borrowers and lenders who have different time duration expectations.

To take an example, let us assume that a bank needs to repay Rani's deposit in September. But the loan it gave to Raja is coming up for repayment only in October. Not to worry, Prem will be repaying his loan in September, which can be used to repay Rani.

Even if the bank cannot find another loan maturing in September, it can bridge the gap by borrowing from other banks, financial institutions and even the Reserve Bank of India. Such an option is not available for a small saver who cannot access institutional money."

Chatur "Now I am starting to realize how complicated it is to lend money on your own."

Kuber "Wait till you hear more; the story is still not complete."

Kuber continues, "I eventually managed to find Diwaaliya Gupta who satisfied all the conditions and gave him the money. For the first couple of months, Diwaaliya was able to pay interest amount diligently and I was starting to feel proud of my selection.

However, a year later Diwaaliya ran into issues. His business had collapsed, he had no cash flows and, he requested me to grant him another two years to repay the money. I was not happy about this and decided to take Diwaaliya to court. However, my lawyer advised me that it was simply not worth the time and effort to pursue such a small amount and advised me to reach an out-of-court settlement. You will not believe this Chatur. I have not received my money even today.

The hard lesson that I learnt is that lending is an activity best left to organized institutions like banks.

To summarize, banks perform many basic services – collecting deposits, lending money, underwriting, collection, recovery, etc. All these functions put together is nothing but 'intermediation.' I hope I was able to explain this core concept in detail."

Chatur "Yes, indeed. Thank you, and this is a story I will never forget."

# Having the Cake and Eating it too!

When Chatur was young, he observed that his friends would compare and contrast interest income from deposits that could be earned from different banks in town. He found it strange that banks should pay income on money that people keep with them. He found it even more intriguing that no one seemed to question why banks did this.

He always thought people kept money in banks because it would be safe there. He would often compare this with the bank locker where we pay a fee to banks to keep our valuables safe. So why then would banks pay us interest income when we keep money with them? Was it not like having a cake and eating it too?

He has a chat with Kuber about this.

Kuber explains, "Chatur, if I offered you 10 lakh rupees today, but also offered you an option of receiving the same 10 lakh rupees a year later, which option would you chose?"

Chatur chose the first option without blinking an eyelid.

Kuber "Why did you chose the first option?"

Chatur "This is because a bird in hand is worth two in a bush. I mean money in hand is better than money coming in later. I can use that money to buy a phone, a bike or even a house. In addition, there is no guarantee I would receive this money a year later, which leads to uncertainty. What if a coronavirus like situation were to come about again?"

Kuber laughs "Exactly! However, let me change the rules a bit. What if I were to offer you 11 lakh rupees a year later?"

Chatur "Oh! That makes it interesting. I may think about the second option if I am being compensated for the risk of foregoing the money now."

Kuber "Great point; you have now learnt about the time value of money. Money has time value, and therefore you need to offer an interest rate to compensate the lender for forgoing his money."

Chatur "Sure, but what does this have to do with banks paying us interest?"

Kuber "Banks do safeguard our money – there is no doubt about it. However, what is interesting is they do not keep our money idle. They lend that money to other individuals and companies and make an income out of it.

Bachat Bank may pay a depositor 5% interest income on his deposits but will lend the same money at 8% interest rate to another individual or a company. In this example, the bank made a net income of 3%. This means banks are actually benefitting from money deposited by savers and not merely safeguarding it.

You may have heard someone mention that banking is a 'spread' business and walked away feeling confused and irritated. The spread is simply the difference of 3% that the bank earned in the above example. The difference between 8% that the bank earned on lending money and the 5% interest it paid on its deposits. It is as simple as that.

In newspapers, you may have read about savings ratio of a country and its criticality. If a country has to grow and flourish, companies will need capital to build and grow their business operations. Banks are key suppliers of such capital. The banking system can provide this capital only if they collect deposits. They can collect deposits only if people save money. Now you can clearly see the linkage here.

When banks give loans, companies will subsequently deploy that money to establish new plants. This will lead to economic expansion and more importantly, new job creation."

Chatur "Wow, Kuber, what a wonderful explanation!"

Chatur continues, "Now I understand why we treat our depositors like god all the time. If depositors are not happy with our service levels and quality, they will take their deposits to a different bank and Bachat Bank will lose market share."

Kuber "Excellent point."

He continues, "Even the smallest of the depositors is important to us and let me explain the reason for this. Tell me what proportion of your salary income is in savings account and why?"

Chatur "I keep at least six months' salary in my savings account to meet emergencies and also to make my bill payments, which includes power, water and telephone bills."

Kuber "Correct. Now imagine millions of such savings accounts coming together in aggregate. They are invaluable for a bank given the low interest expense that it pays for them relative to term deposits. Such small savings accounts will therefore help increase the spread income."

Chatur "But what is the difference between a savings and a term deposit account?"

Kuber "In a term deposit account money cannot be withdrawn before the term expires. For example, if a deposit is for 12 months, the depositor cannot withdraw money until the 12 months is complete. But it also generates higher interest income for the depositor.

On the other hand, a savings deposit is an account, which can be used to withdraw money whenever one desires. It can be used to pay for all the routine expenses. This is also an account where people park money for emergencies like you just mentioned. As a result, banks pay lower interest expense on savings deposits compared to term deposits."

Chatur "Thanks, Kuber. That was really an eye opener for me."

# Chatur Moves to Head Office

After spending more than five years working with Kuber in the branch, Chatur moves to the head office. During those five years, he rotated between various departments, learnt about different banking-related functions, and contributed a lot to the branch profitability by improving productivity and customer service. In fact, Kuber's branch was amongst the top 10% when measured by revenue and profit growth.

Chatur also manages to complete his higher studies and gets himself a specialization in banking studies by undertaking an online course. His education profile is now also good enough for him to move forward and assume higher responsibilities.

Kuber was so impressed by his work that he felt it was not proper to retain him in the branch any longer – he knew Chatur was hungry, ambitious and that he was going to achieve bigger things in life. He happily allows Chatur to move to Head Office.

Chatur becomes the head of consumer banking within five years of joining the head office. During these five years Chatur gets married and has two kids. His parents relocate from their village to stay with him. They all now stay in a nice house which Chatur purchased by taking a mortgage loan. A mortgage loan is a loan given to buy or construct a house.

The consumer banking team was comprised of about a hundred team members. It was one of the most important departments in the bank and contributed a decent portion to bank's profits. Some activities of consumer banking division include credit and debit cards, retail deposits, auto and personal loans, mortgage loans, locker facility, insurance and investment products and wealth management.

When Kuber visits him at the head office one day after a long time, what impresses him most about Chatur is his continued curiosity and willingness to learn. Chatur would approach every subject with a beginner's mind, which is so necessary to challenge the status quo.

For example, on the day Kuber visits him, Chatur and his team are preparing for the annual investor day. The investor day is an event when every department head – along with the CEO – presents his respective business strategy to the investor community.

When Kuber is in Chatur's cabin one of the senior members of Chatur's team, Gyanav, enters the cabin to brief Chatur about the preparation. Kuber was witness to the following conversation between them.

Gyanav "Sir, we are good to go for the investor day. I have checked every item in the presentation and everything seems to be fine."

Chatur "Thanks, Gyanav, But I would like to spend an hour or two today in the evening on this."

Gyanav "Sir, we do this event every year. I am sure I have taken care of everything. There is no need for you to review it."

Chatur "Gyanav, I know that we have looked at the presentation content several times. However, I would still like us to review it once more as if we are seeing it for the first time. This way we can identify gaps in our thesis much better and look at it more from an investors' view point."

Gyanav "Understood. Let's do this in the evening."

Kuber comments, "Chatur, we did very well last financial year and our profits are trending in the right direction."

Chatur "That is true. However, we have to keep working hard to keep this momentum going. We are still way behind our optimal potential. Our bank recently completed a benchmarking exercise measuring us against competition, which shows good room for improvement."

Later that evening after work, Kuber spends some time with Chatur and his family by having dinner with them. The following day he departs from the head office.

# Those Scary Words: NPAs and Capital Adeqauacy

In Chatur's team, there is a junior whose name is Arya, who reminds Chatur of himself. Arya is curious, hardworking and ambitious like Chatur. He is willing to grab time with Chatur and other senior members whenever possible to learn and debate about banking-related topics. In many ways, Chatur sees a younger version of himself in Arya.

Arya had seen words such as NPAs and capital adequacy appear countless number times in the business section of his newspaper and was curious to know more about these terms. Chatur suggested that he speak to Jokhim Das, who worked in the risk department of Bachat Bank. Arya decided to set up a meeting with Jokhim, and they had the following conversation.

Arya "Hello, Jokhim. Thanks for your time. How are you doing?"

Jokhim "Thank you, Arya. I am doing well. Please tell me how can I be of help to you?"

Arya "Jokhim, I have seen complicated words such as NPAs and capital adequacy constantly appearing in the newspaper. I would like to understand these terms better."

Jokhim "Sure that is not a problem at all. Let us start with NPAs. NPA is an acronym for non-performing asset. This refers to loans given by banks, which borrowers have not repaid. Since they are not being repaid, they are called non-performing assets. Typically, NPA is always measured as a ratio. For example, a NPA ratio of 5% means that out of every 100 rupees worth of loans that a bank has advanced, borrowers worth 5 rupees have not repaid their money.

Arya "That is quite clear. However, why do some borrowers not repay their loans?"

Jokhim "That is an interesting question and let me try answering this through an example. Let us assume you borrowed 10 lakh rupees from our bank for some personal spending. Let us also make an assumption that for some unforeseen reason you lost your job."

Arya "What!"

Jokhim laughs, "I did not mean to scare you. I was just trying to give you an example."

He continues, "The bank expected you to repay the loan amount in monthly installments from your salary account. However, you have no income because there is no job, and therefore no ability to service the loan.

We can extend this example to companies. Let us assume that a company took a bank loan to start a soap factory. The factory was built in two years and the company started producing the soaps. unfortunately the demand for the company's brand of soaps was less than expected.

Therefore, the incoming cash flows from the sale of soaps was not good enough to cover all the costs and repay the bank loan. In such a case, the company will not be able to repay the loan.

These are just two examples and there can be countless such examples of why a borrower is not able to repay. Also, please note that whenever there is an economic crisis, the NPA ratio shoots up. This is because companies are not only facing weak demand for their products but they are also looking to reduce the number of employees.

The reduction in demand leads to weak cash flow for the company while the reduced headcount will leave people jobless. Therefore, both the company and their employees may default."

Arya "Thank you, that was useful. What does a bank do when it faces repayment issues?"

Jokhim "The bank will try its best to collect the money back. If the collection efforts fail, the bank will eventually write off whatever money it is not able to collect, which will negatively affect its profits. In some cases, the NPA ratio can be so high that it can wipe out the capital of the bank itself."

Arya "I read about capital wipeout in the newspaper. Would it be possible to explain this term?"

Jokhim "Sure why not. Again, let me try to explain taking an example. Let us assume that Bharat owns 100% of Bachat Bank and Bharat has put in 100 crore rupees worth of capital. With this amount of capital, the bank was able to give loans worth 500 crore rupees. For some reason, the NPA ratio reaches 30%, which would mean that 150 crore rupees out of 500 crore rupees worth of loans are bad loans. In such a case, the amount of loss is more than the 100 crore rupees worth of capital. This means the capital is simply wiped out."

Arya "That was a wonderful example, Jokhim. I don't have any more questions on NPAs. What about the capital adequacy ratio?"

Jokhim "Let us understand the concept first. The regulator for the banking sector is the central bank, which in India is the Reserve Bank of India. The central bank will insist that banks have to maintain a minimum level of capital at all times. This is because banks are collecting deposit money, which is made of savings from millions of households. Therefore, if the banking system were to collapse, it will also wipe out the savings of its depositors.

In addition, banks are very important vehicles in any economy and the main driver of growth and development. The collapse of a banking system can have widespread consequences."

Arya "That is awesome information. I never thought about it this way."

Jokhim "It is always important to understand the concept behind any ratio. Now, let us understand the Capital Adequacy ratio itself. In our earlier example, Bharat had put in capital of 100 crore rupees and the bank had a loan book size of 500 crore rupees. In the capital adequacy ratio calculation, the numerator is the capital and the denominator is the loan book. Therefore, the ratio will be 20% in our example.

Now let us assume that the central bank insists that the capital adequacy ratio cannot go down below 15%. In such a case, the bank will not be able to lend more than 670 crore rupees, another 170 crore rupees above its existing loan book size of 500 crore rupees, which will bring the capital adequacy ratio to about 15%.

Banks make many fine adjustments in the capital adequacy ratio calculation. For example, they adjust the loan book by providing different weighting to different categories of loans. Unsecured loans like credit cards will carry higher risk weighting given their high-risk profile while secured loans like housing loans will carry lower weighting. Safe loans such as loans given to Government and Government-related entities will also attract lower risk weighting."

Arya "It could not have been explained in a simpler manner. I really appreciate your time and effort. One last item to check with you is on net interest margins."

Jokhim "Sure, the spread that a bank makes between its lending rate and deposit rate is the net interest margin. So if the bank lends at 8% and pays an interest rate of 5% on its deposit funding, the difference of 3% is its net interest margin."

Arya "That seems super simple. How do policy rates impact these margins?"

Jokhim "That is a great question. Policy rates are set by the central bank, which banks use as benchmark to set lending and deposit rates. If the policy rates go up, these rates go up and vice versa.

Now the interesting thing is that banks collect three types of deposits – term deposits, savings deposits and current accounts. The mix of such deposits in a bank's balance sheet will determine its profitability when policy rates move. The last two deposits – savings and current accounts – are less sensitive to policy rates compared to term deposits.

Current accounts are usually transaction-based bank balances used by companies on which banks do not pay any interest. Similarly, savings accounts are used by individuals, which provide convenience by allowing transactions like withdrawal, debit card transactions and transfers. Therefore, interest expense on savings accounts is less variable to policy rates.

In a term deposit, money is blocked for the duration of the deposit. Such deposits do not allow for any transactions, and therefore interest rates are higher when compared with savings or current accounts. The interest rate on a term deposit moves in tandem with policy rates. The lending rates will also move in line with policy rates.

Now let us look at what happens when policy rates move. When the policy rates move up, lending rates will rise while deposit rates on only term deposits will rise, causing banks' profits to increase. This is because, as already explained, rates on some deposits such as current and savings accounts do not change much.

However, when the policy rates are moving down, the lending rates will reduce, while deposit rates on only term deposits will go down, causing banks' profits to reduce."

Arya "You could not have explained them in simpler terms. It was very clear. Thank you again. Have a good day."

Jokhim "Glad to be of help, have a nice day."

# Online Banking: A Reality Check

Arya observes it is now possible to buy almost everything online. He wonders if banking services would also completely go online one day. He remembers how his father would spend hours in the village branch chatting about politics, sports and many other things with the bank staff, who were all quite close to him. The actual transaction itself would not take more than five or ten minutes. What would happen to that social fabric and personal touch if banking were to go online?

Many banking functions have already gone online, including parts of loan sanctioning, which is quite process intensive. Transferring money between accounts can be done within seconds and is easier when compared with issuing a cheque or doing a cash transaction. Similarly, balance checks, account statement generation and many other routine things are all available online now.

Arya remembers how his parents treasured the 'bank passbook,' which was religiously bound and more valuable than any other book in the house. However, this has already become a relic. Who cares when you can simply download the account statement directly from the internet and even print it if required?

Could banks end up shutting down all their branches which would free up real estate for other productive purposes? Arya is curious to understand the end game of online banking. He sits down with Chatur one evening to understand this better.

Chatur "You are right to be curious about online banking and its impact on conventional banking. We had commissioned a consulting firm to get us some research on online banking. The findings of that study suggest that a multi-channel offering is the best way going forward. This means banks will have to combine branch banking with online banking. They cannot completely do away with their branch networks."

Arya "But why? When almost everything can be done online, why would people want to use branches?"

Chatur "Well, human behavior can be complex. When VCR and DVD players came around, we all thought cinemas would go out of fashion. Who would want to go to the theatres when you can watch the whole movie at a much lower cost sitting at home? However, cinemas did survive because of the experience that they offer.

In the world of banking, having a physical presence is even more critical than cinema halls. If we do not have a physical presence, it will create a trust deficit amongst our customers as they have parted with their lifelong savings. They want to ensure that their money is safe and when they see a branch up and running in their neighborhood, it reinforces this trust factor. This is particularly true with the older generation who still prefer to visit the branch although they are well aware of online banking."

This intuitively made sense to Arya. When we see a branch close to us, it is an instant reminder that the bank is up and running and that our money is safe as compared to something running entirely online where everything seems to be happening in the background and transparency seems to be lacking. Another factor affecting trust is the danger of online accounts getting hacked and money disappearing overnight.

Chatur continues, "By the way, a multi-channel offering is not very different to other businesses. Take the case of electronic retailers who distribute their products through multiple channels because this offers many advantages over a purely online platform.

For example, when someone purchases a product directly from an electronic retailer's website rather than from an aggregator like Amazon, the after-sales servicing, product returns and repair and maintenance become easier. All one has to do is simply visit the nearest outlet of that electronic dealer.

Also, keep in mind that a physical outlet is a great way to advertise the product. The customer can touch and feel the product and also compare and contrast features of different brands, which will lead to a better purchase decision for him.

Another advantage that a multi-channel offering provides is the speed of service. Let us assume Apple is launching a new iPhone. A dealer with both online and offline platforms can deliver the product quicker when compared with a purely online platform. The customer can order the phone online and opt to collect the same from the nearest outlet rather than wait for the company to deliver it to him."

Chatur continues "A Key advantage of branch banking is that is allows us to cross sell products."

Arya "I have heard about cross selling many times. What exactly does it mean?"

Chatur "You would have gone to a store and ended up buying more than what you wanted because the sales person sold you those things. Do you recall such any such an incident?"

Arya "Of course, it has happened to me so many times. Only last week I went to buy a mobile phone but ended up buying the latest HD TV and also the latest Bluetooth speaker. The salesman marketed them quite well, I must say."

Chatur "There it is. That is one example of cross selling. In the world of banking, we assess all the different financial requirements of our customers and then try to cross-sell products. This may include a life insurance policy, vehicle insurance and investment-linked products."

Arya "What are investment-linked products?"

Chatur "Let me explain how an investment-linked product works with an example. We all know it is good to have some money invested in stocks and shares, which will help diversify our savings. At the same time, the universe of stocks available in the market is quite large and it can be time consuming and difficult for anyone to analyze and select single stocks. Banks like us operate mutual funds, which invest into stocks on behalf of its customers. Such funds are managed by professional fund managers."

Arya "Clear; by the way, how large is the Indian banking system when it comes to number of branches?"

Chatur "India has one of the largest branch networks in the world with more than 120,000 bank branches. State Bank of India, the largest Indian bank, itself has more than 20,000 branches. The Indian banking system is one of the largest employment generators in the country.

However, if you look at branches per every 100,000 units of population, we are not amongst the highest. For example, the number of branches per unit of population in the US is twice that of India. Therefore, it is important to keep the population in mind while comparing the number of branches across countries."

Arya "Super, thank you for all the insights."

# The House of Cards

One-day Arya's wife tells him that she is tired of everyday routine and wants a change. Arya suggests that they all travel together to a new place and enjoy a nice break. They scout for destinations and eventually decide on United States where Arya's brother already lived. This would make easier it for them to navigate in a new country.

Arya knows that the currency in circulation in the United States is US$ and he needs to convert his rupees into US$ to be able to spend money in the US. They have plans to spend nearly two weeks in the United States, and would thus require a decent amount of US$ to meet all the expenses over that time-period.

Arya faces two issues here. First, he needs to convert his INR into US$. Second, he is worried about carrying US$ in cash with him due to security and theft issues. He thinks that the best way to solve the problem would be to use his credit card, but he has a few questions about the credit card business itself.

Arya has always paid his credit card bills on time, and therefore, never paid any interest on any outstanding due amounts. He only paid a small credit card-related fee. He wonders how then banks make money on credit cards.

Chatur suggests that Arya speak to Shrey on this. Shrey heads the cards division of the bank and reports to Chatur. Arya sets up a call with him.

Arya "Hi Shrey, you know my credit card history. I get about 30 days of credit when I incur an expenditure on my credit card. However, since I always pay my dues on time, I do not pay any interest. I enjoy credit for 30 days and the bank does not earn any income from me, save for a small fee. Then how in the world do you people make money from this business?"

Shrey "Good question, Arya. Let me explain."

Shrey "Every time you use your credit card at a merchant's place, the merchant pays the issuing bank a fee, which is based on the value of the transaction. The issuing bank is the bank which has issued the credit card."

Arya "Fair enough. However, why would a merchant not accept cash in place of credit cards if he has to pay a fee to the banks?"

Shrey "For customers, a credit card provides a lot of convenience. The credit card holder does not need to carry loads of cash with him. He also gets about a month in credit, like you already mentioned. He can use the card in international locations without worrying about foreign exchange and security-related issues.

Imagine this. If you carry US$ to the United States, you need to carry loads of them which exposes you to safety and security issues. However, when you swipe a credit card in the United States, the bank automatically purchases US$ on behalf of you and pays the vendor the required amount. The bank will later settle with you in rupees when the card credit payment is due. So, if you spend 1000 US$, you will be billed around 73,000 rupees using the current exchange rate.

There are also other fringe benefits, which I will describe later. Given all the benefits I mentioned, a customer who has a credit card is more likely to transact with a merchant who accepts a card transaction.

Do you see the point now? If a merchant does not accept credit cards, he will lose market share to a competitor who is willing to accept them. In essence, the merchant is hoping to maintain market share or even increase it at the expense of a small fee he pays to the bank."

Arya "Clear like a crystal now."

Shrey continues, "Banks also generate interest income from late payment of credit card outstanding amounts. You are a wrong example for this since you always pay on time. However, some people will not pay on time and the bank will charge interest on such a delayed payment.

The interest rate on late payments on credit cards can go up to 30% per annum, which is a hefty amount. The interest rate is high because credit card is an unsecured facility. An unsecured facility is a facility where there is no collateral or security for the bank to fall back on if the borrower is not able to repay.

A secured facility is a loan which is collateralized – examples are mortgage loans and auto loans. Mortgage loans are granted to buy or build a house, and the house becomes the collateral. Similarly, in an auto loan, the car itself is the collateral.

To reduce the risk, banks also put a cap on credit card spending. The amount of money that one can spend using a credit card is usually limited to a certain percentage of monthly income, which will help restrict unlimited spending and reduce default risk for the bank."

Arya "Can you explain those fringe benefits now?"

Shrey "Sure, why not? In order to win market share in credit cards, banks will try to offer extra benefits to make their cards attractive.

One benefit is buyback in which credit card holders get back a certain percentage of money they spend using their card. Another benefit is discounts where users will get a discount if they buy products from a particular vendor. For example, all purchases made from Amazon above a certain amount could be made to attract a 5% discount. Such an arrangement is mutually beneficial to the card issuer, the user and the vendor.

Another popular program is air miles, which is directly linked to the amount of money spent using the cards. The accumulated miles can be redeemed to buy an air ticket in specified airlines. Some cards also allow users to access airline lounges, which is another important fringe benefit."

Arya "Great, what is MasterCard and Visa card then?"

Shrey "These are the companies who own the technology that enables banks to process a credit card. When a customer swipes the card, the whole transaction happens in a matter of seconds. The system will check if the card spending is within limits, will verify the transaction PIN, check for any suspicious activity and then process the transaction in those few seconds.

MasterCard and Visa Card also get a share of the fees that the merchant pays to the bank. The issuing bank collects the fees from the merchant and pays a certain percentage of this fee to MasterCard or Visa Card."

Arya "Excellent, thanks. I always wondered about the difference in credit and debit cards."

Shrey "Sure, when you use your debit card, the bank is not offering you a loan. The bank is simply taking the money from your savings account. On the other hand, when you spend using your credit card, the bank is giving you a short-term interest-free loan – usually for about 30 days. When those 30 days expire, the bank will charge an interest income on the unpaid credit card balance until it is settled.

Therefore, a debit card offers you only convenience while a credit card offers you convenience as well as a short-term interest-free loan."

# Chatur Becomes CEO in a Challenging Environment

After spending fifteen long years at the bank, Chatur is promoted to the position of CEO of Bachat Bank. Under Chatur's supervision, the consumer banking division had grown and matured, and was now one of the biggest contributors to the overall profitability of the bank. It was a crowning moment in a glittering career. Arya did well for himself and became the head of Treasury. The Treasury function in a bank takes care of cash, liquidity and risk management.

However, there was still miles to go as far as Chatur was concerned. He now had to broaden his exposure and knowledge away from consumer banking into other areas such as wholesale banking, treasury and other functions. However, nothing was beyond his prowess and capabilities, and the appointment confirmed the faith and the trust that the Board of Directors reposed in him.

The 2008 financial crisis and the subsequent aftermath brought plenty of changes in its wake, which have implications on profitability and capital levels.

There is now a new accounting standard for booking loan losses when a customer defaults. An accounting standard specifies the treatment which companies have to follow while accounting for certain things so that reporting is uniform and standardized across the industry.

For example, prior to the 2008 crisis, banks would book losses only after a borrower expressed his inability to repay.

However, regulators realized that this took time because typically distress lags the onset of a crisis.

Take the example of Covid-19 crisis. Many companies will continue to service debt by digging deep into their savings. However, once the savings pool is depleted, companies will start to experience cash flow issues and start defaulting on payments. Therefore, the lag between the onset of a crisis and actual distress can be in months or even in years in some cases.

The new accounting standard will force banks to book expected loss rather than actual losses. Banks will now have to review every borrower in the portfolio, estimate losses and book them immediately rather than waiting for the actual default to occur. They will have to deploy new systems and processes to make such an estimate more robust.

On similar lines, regulators have forced banks to hold more equity capital in their balance sheets. A banks can raise regulatory capital in the form of equity, perpetual bond instruments or subordinated debt. One of the main differences between equity and debt is that while debt has a set repayment date, equity has no repayment date. Perpetual bonds are hybrid instruments which have characteristics of both equities and bonds. They have no repayment date and are, therefore, similar to equity. But they also pay annual coupons and are, hence, similar to bond instruments. A coupon is the interest income that a bank pays a bondholder. Subordinated debt is nothing but debt, which will be repaid after all other forms of debt have been paid – therefore, that makes them subordinate to other debt.

Equity is simply the money which is attributable to the owners of the bank. There is now a minimum amount of equity capital, which banks need to maintain in the mix of capital (equity + perpetual bonds + subordinated debt), which makes it more challenging.

Banks are spending more money on compliance than ever before so that they can track down money which is routed through banks for all the wrong reasons – terrorism, crime and other illegal activities.

In most countries, the central bank policy is tracked down like never before and used as a signal to judge market performance and outlook. A central bank is an institution which regulates the entire banking system and sets the overall policy framework.

One of the main responsibilities of a central bank is to set an inflation target and also set interest rates, which go hand in hand. Inflation is the pace at which prices rise year after year, and the amount of money supply in the system affects the inflation rate.

Let us take a simple example and let us assume that there is only commodity, apple, in the whole economic system. Let us assume there are 1000 apples and each apple costs 5 rupees, so there are around 5000 rupees in the system. Should we increase the money supply to 10,000 rupees and keep the number of apples constant at 1,000, more money now is chasing the same amount of a commodity causing prices to rise. More importantly, the extra 5,000 rupees may not be equally distributed in the economy. This would mean that the people who got richer would bid up the price and take away the apples leaving the poor with little or no apples. So, it is important to keep inflation in check.

The central bank is able to keep a tab on inflation using different mechanisms. For example, they may increase interest rates to stem inflation. This will make it tougher for people to borrow money and spend. We are more inclined to borrow and spend when interest rate is low. The increase in rates will reduce the amount of money supply in the economy and reduce inflation eventually.

Another thing that a central bank could do is to increase the amount of money a bank has to park with the central bank. This is also called "fractional banking system." Under this system, every bank has to park a certain portion of every deposit with the central bank. This is also called reserve money.

So, if someone deposits 100 rupees with a bank, that bank has to park 10 rupees with the central bank if the reserve ratio is 10% and can lend the remaining 90 rupees. Since banks have to park a fraction of their deposits with the central bank, the concept came to be known as the "fractional banking system." A central bank can regulate the volume of money in the system by changing reserve money. If it feels that there is too much money in the system, it can increase the reserve money or vice versa.

Although not very intuitive, a simple change in such a ratio can lead to a massive change in the total volume of money created in the system. Let us look at this through an example.

If a bank collects total new deposits of 1 million rupees, it can lead to creation of 10 million rupees in new money if the reserve ratio is 10%. However, if the reserve ratio is 20%, it leads to total new money creation of only 5 million rupees, half of the original amount.

So if someone deposits 100 rupees into a bank, the bank will lend 90 rupees after depositing 10 rupees with the central bank as reserve money. This 90 rupees will come back as a deposit into another bank, which will lend out 81 rupees after reserve money. This 81 rupees will come back as a deposit into a third bank, which will lend out 73 rupees after reserve money. This cycle will go on but if you add up the total amount of money that banks gave out as new loans that sum total will be 1000 rupees. Alternatively, if you start with a reserve ratio of 20%, the total amount will add up to 500 rupees.

As Chatur was mulling about some of these things and trying to strategize, he got a call from Kuber.

Kuber "Congratulations, Chatur. Your promotion is well-deserved; you made us and our village very proud."

Chatur "Thank you. Kuber. There is a still a long way to go. In the next five years let us take our bank to even higher standards."

The End